A NOTE TO PARENTS

Reading Aloud with Your Child

Research shows that reading books aloud is the single most valuable support parents can provide in helping children learn to read.

- Be a ham! The more enthusiasm you display, the more your child will enjoy the book.
- Run your finger underneath the words as you read to signal that the print carries the story.
- Leave time for examining the illustrations more closely; encourage your child to find things in the pictures.
- Invite your youngster to join in whenever there's a repeated phrase in the text.
- Link up events in the book with similar events in your child's life.
- If your child asks a question, stop and answer it. The book can be a means to learning more about your child's thoughts.

Listening to Your Child Read Aloud

The support of your attention and praise is absolutely crucial to your child's continuing efforts to learn to read.

- If your child is learning to read and asks for a word, give it immediately so that the meaning of the story is not interrupted. DO NOT ask your child to sound out the word.
- On the other hand, if your child initiates the act of sounding out, don't intervene.
- If your child is reading along and makes what is called a miscue, listen for the sense of the miscue. If the word "road" is substituted for the word "street," for instance, no meaning is lost. Don't stop the reading for a correction.
- If the miscue makes no sense (for example, "horse" for "house"), ask your child to reread the sentence because you're not sure you understand what's just been read.
- Above all else, enjoy your child's growing command of print and make sure you give lots of praise. *You are your child's first teacher — and the most important one. Praise from you is critical for further risk-taking and learning.*

— Priscilla Lynch
Ph.D., New York University
Educational Consultant

For Keith,
who can always make me laugh
— K.S.

For my sister, Dolores
— L.D.

Text copyright © 1995 by Scholastic Inc.
Illustrations copyright © 1995 by Larry DiFiori.
All rights reserved. Published by Scholastic Inc.
HELLO READER!, CARTWHEEL BOOKS, and the CARTWHEEL BOOKS logo
are registered trademarks of Scholastic Inc.

Library of Congress Cataloging-in-Publication Data
Shapiro, Kimberly.
    Funny all over : riddles to read yourself / by Kimberly Shapiro;
    illustrated by Larry DiFiori.
       p.   cm. — (Hello reader! Level 2)
    ISBN 0-590-25951-2
    1. Riddles, Juvenile. [1. Riddles.   2. Animals—Wit and humor.
3. Jokes.]   I. DiFiori, Lawrence, ill.   II. Title.   III. Series.
PN6371.5..S535   1995
818'.5402—dc20   94-39147
                                          CIP
                                          AC

12 11 10 9 8 7 6 5 4 3   5 6 7 8 9/9 0/0

Printed in the U.S.A.   23

First Scholastic printing, March 1995

Funny All Over

Riddles to Read Yourself

by **Kimberly Shapiro**
Illustrated by **Larry DiFiori**

Hello Reader! — Level 2

SCHOLASTIC INC.
New York Toronto London Auckland Sydney

What is black and white and read all over?

A newspaper.

And what is black and white and funny all over?

The funny riddles in this book!
Read them and laugh.

What is gray and blue
and very big?

An elephant holding his breath.

What song does a cat like best?

"Three Blind Mice."

When can you take a pet to a dance?

When it's a bunny hop.

What is black and white and red all over?

An angry zebra.

What kind of dog can jump higher than a house?

Any kind. A house can't jump!

What do you call
a ghost's mistake?

A boo-boo.

What did the cows do when they met?

They gave each other a milk shake.

What kind of cookies do birds like?

Chocolate chirp.

Where do rabbits go after their wedding?

On their bunnymoon.

Why was Cinderella thrown off the baseball team?

Because she ran away from the ball.

What do you call a kitten that eats too much?

A fat cat.

Why can't your nose be 12 inches long?

Because then it would be a foot.

What kind of ball is fun to play with but does not bounce?

A snowball.

What is black and white and lives in Hawaii?

A lost penguin.

What did the elephant bring on her trip?

Her trunk.

What is black and white and has 16 wheels?

A zebra on roller skates.

Why did the chicken cross the road?

To get to the other side.

Why did the turkey cross the road?

To show that he was not chicken.

Why did the rabbit cross the road?

Because the chicken had
his Easter eggs.

What did the dinosaurs do when the Ice Age came?

They went skating!

What kind of sandwiches do sharks eat?

Peanut butter and jellyfish sandwiches.

What is smarter than a dog that can count?

A spelling bee.

What game do rabbits like best?

Hopscotch.

What game does a mouse like best?

Hide and Squeak.

Where was the bear when the lights went out?

In the dark.

What is beautiful, gray, and wears glass slippers?

Cinderelephant.

How can you tell which end of a worm is its head?

Tickle it in the middle
and see which end laughs.
And this is the end of the book!